Dead Tree Scrolls

Volume Two

Gordon Horton

Introduction

She doesn't read poetry. She reads very little.

She read your poetry book. She told me it was very good and might even help someone to heal. So, at her request I will be sending someone a copy of your book.

You write poetry that people can relate to.

And that is enough

A message received from a friend

Hello Again,

I've decided to add to "The Dead Tree Scrolls" this second volume. There are still things to say. I'm not writing as much as I used to, this new job keeps me pretty busy, but I have some stuff I'd like to get out there. I feel that, as long as there is someone who can get something out of my work, I need to keep going. So many have lost so much in this past year or so, but it isn't all bad. One day at a time.

I am starting this volume with a story. One of my oldest and dearest friends is the subject. I have loved this woman since I was a freshman in High School. Truly a "Sister in Spirit". Nila wacante wakiya, mi tankshi. Le taku ceceya.

This piece has four parts. The first I wrote about the early days of our friendship, before we lost touch. Then came the tale of her sorrow and loss. Her story doesn't end here. Like the Phoenix, she is rising from the ashes of her pain. There is much more to her story, It just hasn't been written. I think I'll leave that to her.

I call this, "Sparrow's Odyssey".

Sparrow's

Odyssey

Sparrow's Voice

Fresh and free
With an eye for bones
And a Yen for the silver tooth
Born of Grace and dignity
Strength and resolution
Her heart as big as the Great Outdoors
Her voice, the Springs first Sparrow
Iron on the tiller was the hand that rocked her cradle
The Silver Tooth and The Sparrows Voice a freshman
youth befriended
Friendship's chrysalis
Unconsciously embraced
A glorious year, too soon ended
Gypsy dream crushed
A shattered trio drifted
Embraced by Southern Fields turned Green
She blossomed
Strength and beauty, gifted

Silent Sparrow

The Sparrow's voice is silent
How can she think to sing
Her silent tears wash open wounds
Heartbroken feels the sting
Her southern fields are turning brown
Strength slipping day by day
Soul crushing sorrow fills her heart
Her head is held high anyway
The vigil held in solitude
Preparing for the worst
Weight carried with nobility
Her Green grass seems so cursed
A thousand beams of love and care
Are sent her way by friends
We'll harmonize with Sparrows Voice
Though sorrow never ends

Sparrow's Sorrow

Sparrow's voice is dressed in black
Her song is cracked and bleeding
Sorrow crept into her house
And stole the Green fields breathing
It didn't have to be this way
The orange one failed our nation
He doesn't really give a damn
For those beneath his station
This virus washed his plans away
To rule until he died
He could have saved so many folks
If he had only tried
Her heartstrings torn, Her love is lost
The Reaper makes his choice
With righteous anger do we mourn
I stand with Sparrow's Voice

Sparrow's Strength

Sparrow's Voice was quiet
As her grief drowned out her song
But Sparrows spine is stainless
And her spirit oh so strong
Her family gathered 'round her
And sustained her with their love
Her lost ones watching over
From the heavens up above
You cannot keep a good man down
Or woman in this case
Good Sparrow's standing tall again
And takes each breath with Grace
She's back to working on her guns
And walking everyday
She'll be cracking walnuts with her buns
Before she's done they say
Though friends and family are close by
And Jasper at her base
Look closely friends and you will see
Dried teardrops on her face

She's off and running. Moving forward, one day at a time. It doesn't take much to bring back the pain. Memories are triggered in many ways. This next piece was written on Valentine's Day, With her in mind. Among Others.

Missing Pieces

There's a blank space

In my little house

I can't seem to find what can fill it

The thing that was there

Was thread-worn and bare

But so dear to me and my spirit

How can I find

Once more peace of mind

With my heart oh so empty and broken

It's hard to go on

With my better half gone

My Valentine's words can't be spoken

There has been a lot of sorrow for so many this past year. Loneliness and sorrow. Burned into the spirit by this pandemic. Life goes on. So must we.

Grief

A closing door feels so final
Blocking the light from within
As long as you just stand there staring
The next leg of your journey can't win
Sometimes you've just got to do it
Let go and then just turn around
Somehow, you've got to get through it
A new world is there to be found
Nobody says that it's easy
The easy way is to lay down
It's like running in twelve feet of water
Trying real hard not to drown
Survival ain't no betrayal
It isn't like you closed the door
It is what it is I'm just saying
So get your ass up off the floor
Somewhere another door opens
Just waiting for you to walk by
Another new day, a new morning
To get there you just have to try
One step at a time you can muster
One inch at a time if you must
Just keep moving forward my brother
'Cause only in Life can you trust

Get up and get moving. That was my message here. It isn't easy to move on, because the pain never goes away. All it takes is a song, maybe just an odor of perfume or cologne. Turn a corner and see a favorite spot. Suddenly it's yesterday. No, the pain never goes away, you just learn to live with it.

Memories

The memories of absent friends

Invade your thoughts, it never ends

Pleasant ones, though sad ones too

There's really nothing you can do

To stem the tide and stop your tears

You'd have to banish countless years

You'd lose the joy those years have brought

The lessons all those friends have taught

All the bad times you've been through

These things had their purpose too

So shed your tears, embrace those years

And carry on without your fears

That loved ones lost will fade away

Their light grow dimmer, day-by-day

As long as they're held in your heart

From absent friends we'll never part

Sparrow's Voice is not the only friend who lost loved ones this past year. Unfortunately, the older you get, the faster the folks you know disappear. I too have lost people I love. So have so many others. Some I knew, too many I didn't. This next piece was written to address those losses. A message to survivors.

Death Wish

Mourn me not when I am gone
This body tires of living
The aches and pains of life well lived
Mistakes so unforgiving
I'll miss the loved ones left behind
Family, friends, and lovers
Joys of living, crafting, breathing
Fun beneath the covers
So many things I leave behind
So many more await me
All the ones who went before

Life's never-ending journey
My heart fills, both joy and sorrow
From good byes and from greetings
The ones I mourned are beckoning
Joyous, happy meetings
So mourn me not, as I pass on
Know life is never-ending
All the hurts and sorrows gone
An end to all pretending
This life we live upon this Earth
Is just one big Illusion
Reality is just a dream
One filled with much confusion
Take heart my friends, for soon you'll know
While death here is for certain
The truth of life awaits us all
Just beyond the curtain

Carry On

Memory speaks

With the voices of absent friends

Loved ones

Family

No one wants to be forgotten

Honor their lives with life

Their spirits with laughter

Carry on, and you carry them with you

Its ok to give water to the dead

Just remember to smile about the good times

Life goes on. Every ending has a new beginning. Lest you start to think I've just become a gloomy sort, I have a happy story to insert here. My grandson is getting married. His High School sweetheart no less. I wrote this piece to remind him of another poem I wrote. One that I wrote to his Grandmother. You can find that piece in the first volume of poetry I wrote. It is called "I See You". This piece was written with the love in my heart for this young man, and with all the best wishes I can envision. I call it, "With Love".

With Love

I've known you since your date of birth

I've held your little hand

From tiny little squirming grub

To a strong and fine young man

Tried to show you right from wrong

Examples that I set

To show duty, truth, and honor

Is a sure and solid bet

You haven't always tried your best

Adulting kinda sucks

But you've kept a steady job

So you could have some bucks

You've had some fairly awful days

Life's lessons can be hard

But you're still standing tall my boy

Yes, taller by the yard

And now the next step is at hand

You found The Girl in Birmingham

You chased her till she caught you lad

From where I sit that ain't half bad

Her blonde-haired, blue-eyed siren song

Ensnared your heart

Then held on strong

Long distance love is no small task

You've made it work, you've made it last

Now Wedding bells are ringing true

There's one thing I must ask of you.

Remember Sarah all your life

Like I remember my dear wife

Her beauty on your wedding day

Is something that won't fade away

Through loving eyes she'll always be

This stunning vision you'll still see

They have honored me with a request that I read this piece at their reception.

I've discovered that, for me, Poetry is a voice I can use when I have something to say. Some folks can just be given a subject and come up with a piece to match. I've tried that. It ain't pretty. No, for me it seems to work best when I have something to say.

Anything can light the fuse. Politics, religion, random thoughts, even love. This one came about from reading a series of poems written by a woman named Elizabeth. I believe she's Scottish.

Elizabeth

An Angel's Breath from across the pond
Numb with pain and sorrow
Her lover's death has laid her low
And darkened her tomorrow
Life's filled with lessons we should learn
We can choose to make things better
My heart goes out to Angel's Breath
Though I have never met her

She was quite tickled with this little poem, written in her honor. This next one got a very positive response as well.

Love can Be

A harsh and arid landscape
Baked and broken ground
Water is life
The only moisture for miles around
Encased in a thick and thorny shell
Cactus bites if you're not careful
Love can be like that
But once in a while, the rains come
Filling the hollows
Turning the dry beds back into rivers
If there is enough
The desert blossoms
Breathtakingly beautiful
The desert sprouts life
Fast and furious
Spreading its seeds
Only to lie dormant
Until the rains come once more
Love can be like that

And then

There is a slow and steady drip in a vast cavern

Forming unimaginable castles of strength and beauty in the darkness

Where none can see

Water is life

Like a forgotten seed on fertile ground

Slowly, steadily, building

Until a tree stands in the forest

Strong as an oak

Yet supple as a willow

Love can be like that

Thoughts of relationships I've had, and the one I have. Love can be like that.

A friend of mine commented that my relationship with my wife had "made me". I couldn't totally disagree, but I would say rather that she gave me purpose. Who and what we are is the consequence of decisions we have made. Your path is your own. If you are truly fortunate you may find someone you can walk with. Your paths don't necessarily have to be the same if you're going the same way.

A "Made" Man

There's some say my love "made me"
Well, there is some truth to that
It made me realize where I was
Is just not where it's at
It's lots of fun to suck suds down
And burn the sweet skunk weed
Smoked cocaine in an acid rain
A vision quest, indeed
There's hash of many colors that will blow your mind with ease
Mushrooms and peyote have brought many to their knees
But if you check the mirror
Finding Death there with a grin
Right then and there is where your journey back had best begin
I was on my way back from that place when first I met Miss Pat
Now that we walk together I've grown happy, also fat

Love's Promise

Life's breath taken late
The mismatched pieces, a perfect fit
Apples and oranges
An old school woman with a new age vibe
An aging hippie with a laid-back style
To each their own, the task at hand
No questions asked, no demands
Acceptance unconditional
Trading new lamps for old,
Ties were cut to ride the gypsie's wagon
Trading in shellfish along a storm-tossed coast
Standing fast when Fortune shifted
Going back to find a way forward
Humbled Spirits, taking alms, and Shelter From The Storm.
Fickle Fortune strikes again, he struggles on the ladder
Freedom chained, hard labor wins her Castle.
Freedom beckons and spirit flies
Wolves aren't made for Kennels
Laughter finds his shining eyes
As he runs on heartstrings tether
Returning home when life's breath calls
Two move on together
The Autumn of life is harvest time
She keeps the home fires burning
The road gets old cuz it's long and cold
Heartstring's call coming faster
At the end of the day when the sky turns Gray
Thoughts turn to Alabama
Where old school waits, guarding the gates
A candle in the window

I spoke of my brother in Volume one. At that time I didn't know there would be a volume two. He was known as Poet, for good reason. My brother was an old school biker. A "One Percenter" by the original meaning of the phrase. The poetry he wrote told the story of his lifestyle. He talked about a great many things. Nothing was sacred. I've written a few pieces with him as the subject.

This next one was inspired by the Love every biker feels. Poet's burned as bright as any other. A fire no one can extinguish.

SUGAR BEAR

SHE BEGGED HIM NOT TO GO TO HER
THE KIDS WERE STILL ASLEEP
HE'D PROMISED THEM THIS SATURDAY
AN OATH HE COULDN'T KEEP
HER JET-BLACK SKIN WAS CALLING HIM
THE SIREN CALL TOO STRONG
AND SO HE WENT TO DO WITH HER
WHAT SOME WOULD SAY WAS WRONG
HE STRIPPED THE COVERS OFF HER FORM
WHERE SHE AWAITED HIM
AND SLOWLY STROKED HER SMOOTH BLACK SKIN

WAITING TO BEGIN

HE BATHED HER GENTLY, LOVINGLY

NO CREVICE WENT UNDONE

LUBED HER UP AND FED HER

FIREWATER NINETY-ONE

HE STRADDLED HER WITH URGENCY

THEN SLOWLY TURNED HER ON

THE RHYTHM OF HIS MOVEMENTS

TELLING HER THEY'D SOON BE DONE

HE GAVE HER THEN A MIGHTY THRUST

THAT GOT HER MOTOR RUNNING

A THROATY ROAR, HE HEARD HER PURR

THE THROTTLE HE WAS GUNNING

A WARM AND SUNNY SATURDAY

IN WINTER CAN'T BE WASTED

A RIDER'S MISTRESS IS HIS RIDE

SUCH FREEDOM MUST BE TASTED

There's more than one kind of love, and no limit to how much you can feel.

In the early 80s my brother performed a piece of his work for a very small audience. I have tried in vain to find a copy. On that day, his was the voice of prophecy. On the 6th of January in 2021 something very much like the story he told took place in Washington DC. Since I couldn't find the poem he wrote I have tried to recreate something of the feeling it generated in this piece. I cannot take full credit. It was his story. Though I have added my own flavor and twist and given it a more positive outcome, I felt him at my shoulder as I was writing. I can only say that this poem was written by Poet and his brother Flash. I call it,

Poet's Ghost

Rolled out from California

With the big iron on his hip

Had all his brothers with him

As they gave the law the slip

Sent my manifesto to

Fox News channel 13

It's time these politicians learned

What "We the People" means

They rolled on through the desert

In the dark and just for fun

Invited others to join in

This Revolution Run

It wasn't just the MAGA nuts

The donkeys too must go

They sold us out, these dirty rats

Their colors true did show

They filtered in from everywhere

Bikes and truckers too

The last of all the free men

The bold, the brave and true

He led them into Washington

And in the dark of night

They overran the capital

Without a single fight

When morning came, this ragtag band

They took the Senate too

Their numbers were a million strong

They bled red, white, and blue

He had them ring the Whitehouse

Bikes and trucks were ten yards deep

The staff was taken by surprise

The President, still asleep

No one had a chance to run

They didn't have a clue

No one knew for sure

Just what this crazy man might do

They gathered up the House

And then they brought the Senate down

He knocked and asked the President

To join them on the lawn

He wasn't there to bring U.S. down

But lift U.S. up instead

He read my manifesto then

Drilled it in their heads

He got them all to promise

That this plan would be done

Then he looked them in the eye

And told them just for fun

If you don't follow through on this

You'll see me one more time

Then he shot the red groups leader

Just to prove he didn't mind

The army had troops closing in

They came from North and South

He sent his people East and West

News came by word of mouth

They scoured all the land for him

He gave them quite a fright

But no one found a Trace

He simply vanished in the night

My manifesto was soon ratified

A new democracy was born

Although taking time to grow

It started out that very morn'

They were afraid to face him

And the free men at his side

They knew this massive movement

Would give them no place to hide

They put a price on this man's head

No matter what they say

But where did Poet get to?

It's a mystery to this day

Wrote this one with my grandchildren on my mind. You might not notice, but they don't miss much. Be careful, they remember what they see.

Mirrors

So precious are the little ones
A gift that keeps on giving
All innocence and honesty
So sweet, and so forgiving
They laugh and sing and play all day
They bring us what they find
The Wonders in this great wide world
That occupy their mind
The coolest rock, a muddy frog
A bee that gathers honey
Delight in their shining eyes
Infectious and so funny
If only we could stop time here
When they still enjoy our talks
Before they get things figured out
From watching us like Hawks

Time marches on, and in time, so will they.

Every day is a new beginning. Nothing says you have to keep going in the same direction.

The Fountain

The Sun Rises on a new day

There are those who won't embrace it

Clinging to the scrapes from yesterday's sidewalk

Saving the stitches from their broken hearts like a

medal of honor

Like a road map to their future

Scars are the textbooks from our freshman year

Not our diploma

You can't put new wine in old bottles

But you can melt them down and blow new glass

Acquiring fresh skills along the way

The perpetual classroom is a fountain of youth

Stay thirsty

Had a conversation with a friend of mine about his struggles to quit smoking. It brought back my own struggle. We all have our demons.

Turnabout

Addiction is real

Doesn't matter what kind

If the shit's in your blood

Or just in your mind

Searching the floor

For a little White Rock

Knocking three times

On the wall when you stop

Light up a smoke

A nail for your coffin

Finding a vein

For the pain that needs stopping

There are many who have

An unquenchable thirst

A mind gripping longing

That brings out the worst

A long way the wrong way

Whiskey bent and hellbound

Don't let people tell you

You can't turn around

Folks just can't travel

Too far to come back

At some point those demons

Will fall off your back

And if you don't make it

The truth will be found

The wrong road was taken

But you did turn around

I've written a number of poems about the struggle to succeed, but what is success? Some want to be rich. Some want to be famous. Some will be happy with just enough. There are those who would be thrilled by finding their next meal. Not everyone will approach the struggle with honor.

Charities Choice

They cry for alms

Yet are they truly poor?

Con men, grifters, and cheats,

Wearing coats of anxiety and despair.

Applying layers of homelessness and hunger

as they park their Lexus in a hidden corner.

Out of sight, out of mind.

From the corner where they beg

Taking food from the hungry

Stealing Hope from the hopeless

Living large on the kindness of strangers

The red tide of capitalist royalty have unleashed a

flood of need

The Orange Blossom Special undermining the
foundation of economic stability

Even now, when his branch has been pruned from
the tree.

Sowing hatred and division, casting blame.

All the way to the ground.

Refusing to acknowledge the vision in the mirror.

No one wants to take food from their plate to feed a
glutton,

But most will gladly feed a starving family.

How do you tell the difference?

A skillful artist, seeking to be paid for his rendition of
despair.

A desperate stranger searching for hope.

How do you know which?

A gift of love does not condemn the giver.

You can only follow your heart.

One random act of kindness at a time

These next pieces reflect my thoughts on the pursuit of the American dream.

The Grail

The Quest for the Holy Grail
A once Noble pursuit
Pilgrims bound by Honor and Duty
Guided by the principles of hard work, dedication,
exemplary performance.
The chalice itself?
Success, no more no less
Open to all, if you rise or you fall,
Determined by the tools on your bench
Not the pads on your knees
The Grail has been taken by Greed
Power hold the keys to the fruits of excellence
Success is measured by the amount of lubrication
applied to Greed's ego
Fueling the fires of self-importance
The Craftsman must play Atlas
While duty weeps for the death of Honor

American Dream

A car in every garage,

A chicken in every pot.

But what about the tents under the bridge?

Who dreams for them?

A thousand-yard stare,

Across a fire built from scraps and deadfall.

Soup from ketchup packets.

Dumpster bread with the mold torn off.

An hourglass where the Hope has run out.

Roasted rat and a Christmas pigeon

The feast at the Fisher King's table

A helping hand looks poised to slap.

Trust is a dream.

Broken hearts still beat

Though broken dreams have died

Unseen Pieces

Lonely extra on an endless stage
Trying to make his mark
Watching the world go by
Always on the fringe
Outside looking in
Watching the lead roles dance and sing
Always in someone's shadow
Countless auditions,
Thanks for stopping by, Next please!
Bigger roles in smaller stories
Never catching on, cancelled.
Looking for that big break.
Missing the point.
There wouldn't be a spotlight
If someone didn't turn it on
The most important parts are played
By people you don't see.
We are all in this together
A puzzle needs every piece
Or you only see what's missing

TANJ

Nobody wants you to sing your song
They only want theirs to shine
Doesn't matter to them if the boat they're riding
Is floating on optical brine.
The suits are well practiced at flashing a smile,
The one that they show to your face.
The minute they think you might cost them a dime
They put someone else in your place
The years that you served, the shed blood, sweat, and
tears.
Are just what the suits think you owe
For their minimum wage and your soul in a cage
With a whip that they crack so you'll go
If you dare to speak out, telling what it's about
They'll cut you right off at the knees
They won't let you run in the shade or the sun
They pretty much do as they please
With a well-filled war chest and a shyster that's best
Degrees written in blood on the wall
A poor man can't win so they wait with a grin
Then they laugh as you starve and then fall

Greed

The suits all want it now,

But it's us behind the plow.

While our cousins in their harness stare in wonder

Incessant frenzy fueled desire

To produce, consume, acquire.

Resting on a razor's edge, you have to ponder

Acquisition tips the scales,

Consumption screaming off the rails

While production figures give the suits their plunder

It's Mother Earth who foots the bill

Taken from her bosom's till

We must balance out the scale or we'll go under

If you can't take it with you,

You don't own it

Acquisition serves no purpose,

But greed

Walmart

The process to get hired was the most intensive I have ever experienced as a truck driver. In most cases, it takes about three or four days to get into your truck and hit the road solo. Not the case with Wal-Mart.

It took a week just to pass the driving test. Say what you want about this company, they were thorough. There were people there with thirty years of driving experience who didn't make it past the first week. Someone commented that it felt like truck driver boot camp. They were not wrong. By the time the morning the final day of the skills test came around you felt like you had accomplished something. It was more than a driving skills test. It was an indoctrination. There was even a morning cheer.

On the morning of the day we *had* to pass, I wanted to encourage and congratulate those of us who made it. So I wrote this piece.

The Summit

We came to test our mettle
Against the blue and gold
Our ages ranged from fresh-faced youth
To grizzled, gray, and old
To sit on Walton's mountain
With the very best of men
And yes, we know their women
Are every bit as good as them
We walked in feeling very sure
We'd stand with all the rest
We didn't know how high the bar
Was placed for this long test
Their uniforms were clean and pressed
Their visage, stern but kind
They took the things we thought we knew
And put them out of mind
They gave us all the answers
So that we could pass this test
So we could join Sam Walton's Crew
And ride among the best

I have found this to be both the hardest and the easiest job I've ever had. Just like the man said. I've written a few poems about this opportunity. A private fleet is a far cry from a trucking company. Do I agree with everything about this job? Absolutely not, but at the end of the day you have to ask yourself this question. Are they paying me enough to put up with it? Say what you want about Walmart, I'm still here. The following poems are part of the reason why.

Respect

A pearl of great price

Denied some 40 years

Earned time and time again

What need have the Suits to show the collars respect

Judgmental bias

Gauged by your own mirror

The window to another's soul

Apples and oranges

And now a giant shakes my hand

Accepts my word

A valued associate

Not a numbered paper

A welcome surprise

Respect

PHDad

Got a dome so slick a wig won't stick

Sporting Goldberg whiskers on his chin

Needs a mentor patch on that clean blue shirt

Got himself a wicked little grin

The gift of gab with a Southern twist

Fitbit riding on his limp left wrist

A claims run is where he likes to spend his time

But if Walmart needs a trainer he steps up to the line

Old school ethics with a stone-cold vibe

But he's really just a marshmallow man inside

Ol' Hammer Hand has a heart of gold

If help is needed, he don't have to be told

Daddy's girls know he's got their back

His sons know who to call if their tail's in a crack

Yeah you'd have to look around to find a better man

He'll stick to his guns and you know where you stand

Better leave his kin alone if you want to make it home

Make no mistake, Thor is bad to the Bone

Gator

Jack be nimble

Jack be quick

But Jack ain't jumping over no dang candlestick

They call The Man Gator on the radio

Where he got that handle, I just don't even know

An old school trucker there can be no doubt

Training Walmart drivers is what Jack's all about

He'll get you in the classroom

Take you out on the road

One thing he won't do is leave you out in the cold

When a child needs a hand

Gator Jack is all in

His Walmart Heart

Shows him where to begin

You can count yourself lucky

If he calls you his friend

One thing you can rely on

Is he'll be there till the end

Yeah, that's what you're gonna find out here in the sticks

A bunch of good ol' boys

Like Gator Jack Hix

This next poem is about a woman I watched work for about thirty minutes. She solved an issue with my on-board computer that no one else knew how to fix. I was so impressed with this woman's level of skill that I wrote her this poem. It took about five minutes, and every word is true.

The Wizard of Walmart

Standing 5'4 with an easy stride
Soft spoken woman with a strong sense of pride
Keen-eyed and swift
Sharp as a tack
The drivers in Kentucky know
She's got their back
Takes up a challenge
As fast as she can
Even did a favor for a Cullman man
Her fingers Grace the keyboard
Like lightning on a stick
Try and catch the action
Ain't nobody else that quick
She'll iron out the problem
That nobody else can find

Solving three more problems
In the back of her mind
I'm just glad she had the answer
For the bind I was in
Now tomorrow is a new day
And my trip can begin
Just thought I'd share this story
Before I depart
Hopkinsville Becky
The Wizard of Walmart

I've got a couple more from "Wally-World" that I'd like to share. One I wrote for the shop. Unfortunately, they know my name all too well. The other is about the Distribution Center I work from.

Breakdown

The mechanics all think that I'm a jinx

"Them rigs ran fine afore ye!"

But when I get behind the wheel

The warning lights just floor me

Amber check this, and red stop that

The AC quits, the tires gone flat

Injectors are knocking like a Dead Man's Bones

The APU needs safety cones

There's no way I could plan these things

The air brakes are squealing like a fat man sings

I hate being brought back in on a hook

So I don't mind writing them a book

Now I know the techs are all just funnin'

They fix it up and get the engines humming

But man they hate to see me coming

With a maintenance list that's 10 lines running

6806

Now that I've been here for some time

There's something I must say

Of all the DC's I've been to

Cullman wins the day

Hopkinsville is pretty close

They've good folks as well

But Cullman's where the home fires burn

These folks are pretty swell

We've got a cop as safety top

Though he can drive a truck

A cop is how he started out

The mindset really stuck

But you won't find a better man

If what you did was right

He'll beat the bush and watch the films

To bring the truth to light

Yeah, Dennis likes to get things done

But in the Walmart way

If you can play the game like that

You might just get to stay

For all the mundane safety stuff

He's got a woman on his side

Belinda has a smile for you

But she'll still tan your hide

Jacob keeps the trucks in line

Jason tells you why

Blue's the boss and I tell you hoss

He's not that bad a guy

Operations is a friendly bunch

Although there is this one

She can be a bit... Snooty

If you wind her up

Just run

The drivers here will make it clear

They'll help you all they can

The shop will keep you on the road

The ROC has got a plan

I have to say I'm glad I got to make it to this

place

Here's where I'll retire

When I step out of the race

Enough about Walmart. For now I'd like to end with a random selection of poems not included in the first volume of the Dead Tree Scrolls. I'm not writing as much, I'm pretty busy these days, but I'm still writing.

Untitled

I haven't had much time to think

Or to write a single word

Working from can to can't see

It's really quite absurd

I'm told my muse is controversy

Ain't been none of that

I hate to think I'd have to leave

This job to get it back

But no, it seems I haven't lost

The knack to make things rhyme

The issue seems to be

That I just haven't had the time

Poetry

Printed words on a single page
A struggle to tell a tale so briefly
Each tale a drop of water in an endless Sea
A short life fills a bucket
How then to tell a tale
Of a life well-lived
A skillful bard skims the surface
Describing the flotsam to gleeful applause
Never plumbing the depths
The heart of the matter, too deep.
Intricate complexity far beyond the understanding of
casual entertainment
And yet, so essential to the story
The bard profits from his swift glance.
Telling the tale, describing the struggles
To the tune of gold on silver
While the driving force is unseen.
Unknown

Pause

A mind awash with a swirling mix of detail

A new deal for an old trade

Essential service on an endless train

The wheels of commerce roll on

An abstract gift waits patiently

For the swirling mist to gel

Waiting for the pattern to fall into place

Laughingly leaping into the fray

To once more create

A dream

Bridges

Understanding grips the ledge
White knuckled
While misguided faith takes the leap
Eyes closed
No easy way down, no soft landing
Understanding seeks to build Bridges
Everyone crossing safely
Their Prophet seeks to fill the void
With the bodies of the people
So the elite can waltz across
Oblivious to the blood on their shoes
Blind Faith, expecting miracles
Leaps to its death
While understanding labors to save them
Against their will
Brow dripping sweat
Calloused hands, dripping blood
Understanding pleads
If you would but open your eyes

Crucifixion

People talk about division
But they multiply the cost
If you mold them in your image
Diversity is lost
The world that we all live in
Has a million things to see
If you paint them all one color
Oh how boring that would be
Can't we just be different?
Does that have to be offensive?
Why can't we disagree
Without being so defensive?
When you yell and point your finger
Shouting out that he's a stranger
Your savior bows his weary head
He knows that he's in danger

Faith

Those who bend their knee at the cross of the
sacrificed God cannot hear the words of their
prophet.
Their Sacred Scrolls, contradictory.
The "unchanging word" twisted beyond the
recognition of he who spoke them.
A thousand variations on a single theme.
A twisted paradigm.
Prayer is a spell cast by those who would burn
witches.
With no understanding of it's power,
No faith in it's gift.
Is it any wonder hypocrisy rules the cult of
Christianity.
The one called Christ weeps in frustration and
dismay at the mockery made of his message, the
violence conducted in his name.
Such violence cannot be conducted in silence.
This is where you will find your salvation

In the whisper of the wind through the trees.

The sound of one hand clapping.

The voice of that which we choose to call,

God.

But you must learn to listen.

Embittered

An orphan on a red Sea

Holding fast to the roots of freedom

Surrounded by delusional hypocrisy

Their Captain holds a match to the Constitution

Waving a red flag

With nothing up his sleeve

Peace bought with Silence is a willing shackle

I stand against a red tide

The growing light of reason

Visible on the shore

Though it seems I stand alone at times

I will not falter

A wave of change is coming

Extended Hand

A conversation is a two-way street.

If there's nothing coming the other way, how do you know the road is open?

If you knock on a door and no one answers, is anyone even there?

If you turn the other cheek and get slapped on the other side at least you have an answer.

How long can you wave an olive branch before it dies?

Sheep in Wolf's Clothing

The easiest person to fool is the man in the mirror.
Someone who validates our desperate need to believe
in that story is our hero.
Most don't have the strength to open their eyes.
To see what's really happening.
A path of destruction is easy to follow. It looks as
though something is being accomplished.
Desperate people want to see things happening,
but a planted seed takes time to grow. Time and care.
For some the truth will only become apparent when
there is nothing left to destroy.
So they dance along behind their pied Piper,
following the trumpets promise of sugarcane and
honey.
Dancing barefoot through the broken glass.
Calling us sheep as they follow their Shepherd.
Straight into the Apocalypse

HEROES

PEOPLE LOVE A FEEL-GOOD SONG.

THEY WANT TO HEAR A FEEL-GOOD STORY.

THEY WANT THE HERO TO PREVAIL.

DRESSED IN ROBES OF GLORY.

THE REAL WORLD DOESN'T WORK LIKE THAT,

IT WON'T TURN OUT THAT WAY.

THE FEW YOU FIND WHO SPEAK THEIR MIND

ARE WRAPPED IN MISTS OF GRAY.

THERE'S NO SUCH THING AS BLACK AND WHITE.

REAL HEROES FEAR THE DANGER.

NO GOOD AND BAD, NO DARK AND LIGHT.

THE TRUTH IS EVEN STRANGER.

NO ARMORED KNIGHT STEPS UP TO FIGHT,

ONE ONLY WORE LACE COLLARS

THERE'S JUST A SOUL WHO KNOWS WHAT'S RIGHT.

WHO WON'T STOP FOR THEIR DOLLARS

THE HERO DOESN'T GET THE GIRL,

THE HEROINE, NO WEDDING.

THEY'RE JUST A FOOTNOTE, IN A BOOK.

A HISTORY WE'RE FORGETTING.

THE ONES THE SONGS ARE ALL ABOUT?

WOULD RATHER NOT HAVE BEEN THERE.

GLORY REALLY AIN'T MUCH FUN.

JUST COLD, AND DEATH, AND DESPAIR

THAT ISN'T WHY THEY MADE THE TRY,

IT WASN'T FOR THE GLORY.

IT WASN'T SO SOME HISTORY BUFF

COULD READ HIS KIDS THEIR STORY.

IT AIN'T NO FUN TO GET THINGS DONE

MERE CHANCE SHOWED US THEIR TRUE GRIT.

THE REASON THAT THEY STOOD THEIR GROUND?

BECAUSE SOMEONE HAD TO DO IT.

Sand Castles

There are those that say drama is the poet's muse

Sound and fury giving voice to outrage

An aching heart to Love's rhythm

Tears to the song of sorrow

Living in the moment of God's whisper

How can you shout

How can you not

Silence makes a whisper bellow

With the voice of that which we choose to call God

In emptiness lie the answers

Acceptance brings clarity

Beautiful sorrow sings to Love's rhythm

Silence the answer to outrage

Big Brother's critics call contentment blind

And yet

Contentment still speaks

In Silence

The Cost

Consciousness comes at cost

The price of being

Many labor a lifetime to open their eyes

Only to wish them shut once more

The sun shines too brightly

For a mind schooled in Shadow

The light of day embraced

Pierce's the heart of darkness

Clarity, a double-edged sword

Cuts the ties that bind

Not a book that you can lend

It has to be bought

You can't force the vision

It has to be seen

You needn't drown to save an anchor

Bait and Switch

Flowery phrases, spoken in hushed tones

In the fragrance of sage and cedar

To the beat of a homemade drum

Rapt sponges soaking it in.

Thirst clarifies the flavor of brackish water

And triples the price

A spiritual Penn and Teller

Holding aloft a crystal star

While their office picks your pocket

Charging the marks all the traffic will bear

For the smoke and mirrors of shamanistic enlightenment.

While the wind whispers

Deep in the forest

Speaking with the voice of ancient trees

The gift of serenity in timeless moments

The cost, only Love

Pop Quiz

This life is a test that I hope to pass
Though I don't always get the right answers.
Despite all our egos, successes, and failures
We are all just singers and dancers
We act out our parts on this world of a stage
Looking for love and a blessing
The things here we have, that we reach out and grab
In the end it's just window dressing
We tell our tall tales as we share our travails
Of our hunt for what ego is masking
This thing that we seek from the shores to the peaks
Has always been there for the asking
The wind in the trees has the answers we need
If we'd stop long enough just to listen
From our mother the earth we can learn of it's worth
The joy of it makes our eyes glisten
The test ain't that bad once the answer is had
Though a lifetime was used in the tasking
When you take that last ride and there's no place to
hide
Are we one? Is the question Life's asking

Reality Check

I have stood on a summit
Looking out over the masses
Thinking myself anchored at the top
Only to step back and find myself
Sprawled in a gutter, fighting for scraps
Looking up at a range of mountains
Rising, successively into the distance
Taller than the one at my back
From which I had fallen
The journey never ends
Keep climbing

Vigilance

Danger lurks
Just beyond the horizon
The Orange one, biding his time
His Cult of personality is strong
We must be stronger
He sits, sowing hatred and division
Unrest, his stock in trade
Casting blame for the world of his creation
Among those who worship at the altar
Are many who bend their knee at the cross of the
sacrificed God
None of them care to recognize the hypocrisy
dripping from their tongue
As 45 lies sprout from their lips
Like grass on the Savannah after the rains come
We cannot rest on our laurels thinking we won
the war
When there are battles yet to be fought
The Orange one lives
And his minions are dancing

Coin Toss

Darkness calls out

Abide with us my pretty

So tempting to answer that call

Heartache, Pain, and Misery urge us

Leave the light and rest

Soothing oblivion

Empty

This is not our fate

To leave the light early

To abandon all for an end to strife

Loss is at once a blow and a lesson

Easy never won the day

Hard are life's lessons

Those that count

Matter

Coins have two sides

Keep flipping

COFFEE

Roses are red

They grow in the yard

I'm still in my bed

'cause mornings are hard

I got to get up

To bring in some bucks

And oh by the way

Poetry sucks

Must.... have.... Coffee

Blame

How could you do this?

They cry with loud voices

You just got me fired!

You had other choices!

My children are taken

My spouse has just left me

I've just been arrested

My bank account's empty

Why blame someone else?

What brought the truth out?

Just who did the things

They're talking about?

An honest man answers

A question with truth

And children don't need

To be under that roof

You cheated and now

Your spouse won't stick around

They cleaned out the bank

And moved clean out of town

You did the deed

And now you're in jail

You sold corporate secrets

And deleted the mail

Wrong is just wrong

Discovered or not

Sooner or later

Uncovers the plot

The guilty blame others

It's really insane

Though they were the culprit

They still cast that blame

Normal

A frozen slice of time
A comfort zone for the suits
A club to which they can deny admission
While they paint the world a somber shade of gray
The 1% who decide
Smiling all the while
Calling this the natural order of life
No time to waste
There is gold to be gathered
And dreams to be crushed
Normal is just a word
And the word is a lie
The natural order of life
Lies in the moment
The subtle dance of sunlight and moisture
Casting rainbows into the sky
The pattern in a snowflake
The texture of freshly frozen dirt
A widow's tears and a mother's laughter
Normal is a mold for Jell-O
Be a funnel cake

Sight

Flaming sunrise 'cross the sky

Majestic eagle's flight

Rainbows on a cloudy day

A million stars at night

The beauty in a woman's smile

A desert cactus bloom

The way your lover brightens up

When you walk into the room

To only get one side of these

Is still an honest blessing

The blurry image on the left

Can only keep me guessing

What will I do when on the right

My vision starts to fade

When details of that starry night

My memory has to trade

The eye is such a miracle

A gift we take as given

It's such an easy thing to lose

No sure thing while we're living

I'm glad that doctors found a cure

An answer for my plight

So I will still be blessed to see

The beauty of starlight

Destiny

People talk about their destiny
Like we don't have a choice
Free will is our destiny
The choice we make, our voice
We have a say in what we do
Just who we want to be
That doesn't mean the universe
Won't guide us in our need
The path we walk is ours alone
The future is our load
We're given choices we must make
At each fork in the road
That great wide road looks mighty good
An easy downhill stroll
That takes us to the mountain's root
No way to reach our goal
To reach the mountains top you see
We have to make the climb
And clear obstructions as we go
Learning all the time
The hard choice tempers spirit's steel
Growth burned into our soul
That guides us to our father's house
When it's our time to go

Thanksgiving Prayer

My heart is heavy this holiday morn'
From loved ones lost and those forsworn.
Yet I have to smile as on I go
Remembering loved ones I still know.
No, they're not all ancestral kin
But they've been there through thick and thin
When times got hard, they've had my back
While siblings just gave me the sack.
These folks have shown me much more care
Than some who's DNA I share.
There's still some family on this list.
They're not all gone, though all are missed.
We may not talk from day to day.
Years might pass along the way
Yet when we talk it's still the same
As when they first found out my name
I cannot doubt that love exists
When I see those names written on that list
So on this day it's thanks I'm giving
For those who passed, and those still living.

Future's Choice

I'm staying out here on the road
Throughout this holiday season
I'm told it's Christmas folly
But I think I have good reason
We've got no little ones at home
It's just the wife and me
No presents waiting Christmas morn'
No reason for a tree
If I can keep this left door shut
And keep these big wheels turning
My wife and I might just get by
On social security's earnings
I never thought I'd be alive
At this late stage in life
With candle's both ends burning
Through heartache, pain, and strife
Imagine my surprise when she came knocking at my door
Ending all those lonesome days
And nights forevermore
You see I have to make the best of time that I can run
So she and I can end our days Together in the sun

Family Christmas

You're once more gathered around the tree

The Mean One bought so merrily

You gathered here from near and far

And pulled a name out of the jar

Scratched your head and thought a bit

To find a gift that just might fit

Now there's a new twist to this game

Because the Girls gift never came

And Patrick's gift? it got lost too

Now they'll get an IOU

But Grandma always pays her debt

The mailman's going to bring it yet

And I'm still out here on the road

Colorado bound with a heavy load

So have some food and laugh a lot

Just leave me an empty spot

Pretend that I've just left the room

Make believe I'll be back soon

When you open your gift try to act
surprised
Merry Christmas folks, I love you guys

This seems as good a place to stop as any. I've made more of an effort in this volume to, "Just do the poem". After all, these pieces are my thoughts and feelings. If you get it there is no need to explain. If not, an explanation would probably not suffice.

Whether or not you understand what I was trying to say, perhaps these words may strike a different cord within you. If you can garner some meaning or comfort from what I've had to say, It has been worth the effort.

Until next time………..

Made in the USA
Middletown, DE
12 October 2021

50179313R00050